A
CHRISTMAS
CAROL
COLORING BOOK

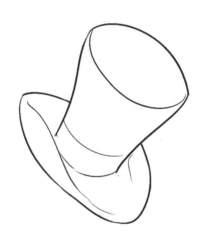

A CHRISTMAS CAROL
COLORING BOOK

MARTIN BUSTAMANTE

SIRIUS

SIRIUS

This edition published in 2024 by Sirius Publishing, a division of
Arcturus Publishing Limited,
26/27 Bickels Yard, 151–153 Bermondsey Street,
London SE1 3HA

ISBN: 978-1-3988-4402-5
CH010163NT

Printed in China

Introduction

First published on 19 December 1843, Charles Dickens' *A Christmas Carol* sold out its first printing by the end of that year and went on to print 13 more times in 1844. It has remained a beloved Christmas story ever since. The timeless tale tells of a selfish man, addicted to money, who is shown the impact and error of his ways—but ultimately allows him salvation. The story set down and crystallized in the minds of Victorian Britons the idea of Christmas as a time for family, gathering, and generosity as well as many of the foods, such as goose and turkey, now indelibly linked with the holiday.

This coloring book takes 45 scenes from the novella and illustrates them, alongside passages from Dickens' text. Use a selection of pencils or markers in a warm and traditional palette along with a dash of Christmas cheer to bring the story and these illustrations to vibrant life.

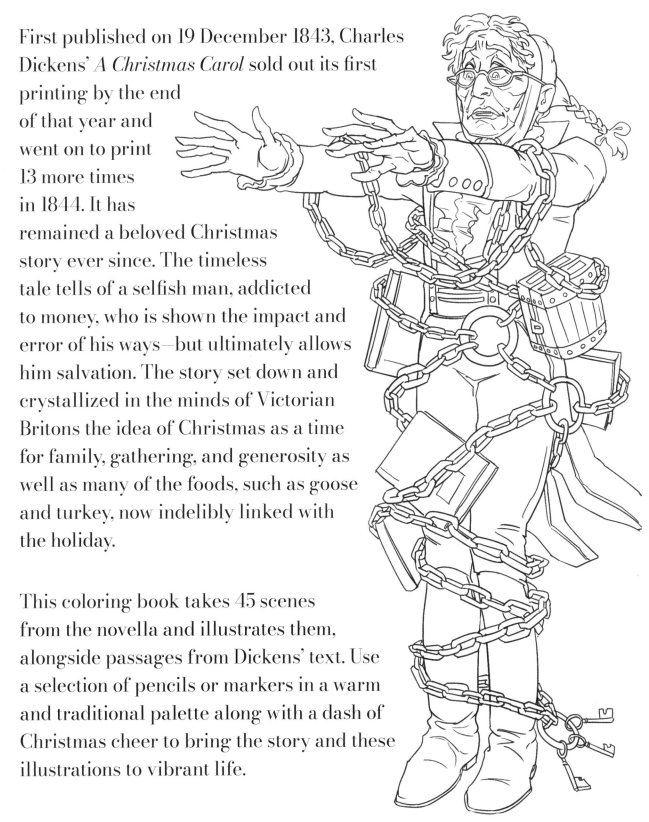

Oh! But he was a tight-fisted hand at the grindstone,
Scrooge! A squeezing, wrenching, grasping,
scraping, clutching, covetous old sinner!
Hard and sharp as flint, from which no steel had ever
struck out generous fire; secret, and self-contained,
and solitary as an oyster. The cold within him
froze his old features, nipped his pointed nose,
shrivelled his cheek, stiffened his gait; made his eyes
red, his thin lips blue and spoke out shrewdly in
his grating voice.

Once upon a time—of all the good days in the year, on Christmas Eve—old Scrooge sat busy in his counting-house. It was cold, bleak, biting weather: foggy withal: and he could hear the people in the court outside, go wheezing up and down, beating their hands upon their breasts, and stamping their feet upon the pavement stones to warm them.

"A merry Christmas, uncle! God save you!" cried a cheerful voice. It was the voice of Scrooge's nephew, who came upon him so quickly that this was the first intimation he had of his approach.

"Bah!" said Scrooge. "Humbug!"

He had so heated himself with rapid walking in the fog and frost, this nephew of Scrooge's, that he was all in a glow; his face was ruddy and handsome; his eyes sparkled, and his breath smoked again.

"Christmas a humbug, uncle!" said Scrooge's nephew. "You don't mean that, I am sure?"

This lunatic, in letting Scrooge's nephew out, had let two other people in. They were portly gentlemen, pleasant to behold, and now stood, with their hats off, in Scrooge's office. They had books and papers in their hands, and bowed to him.

Meanwhile the fog and darkness thickened so, that people ran about with flaring links, proffering their services to go before horses in carriages, and conduct them on their way. The ancient tower of a church, whose gruff old bell was always peeping slily down at Scrooge out of a gothic window in the wall, became invisible, and struck the hours and quarters in the clouds, with tremulous vibrations afterwards as if its teeth were chattering in its frozen head up there.

The brightness of the shops where holly sprigs and berries crackled in the lamp heat of the windows, made pale faces ruddy as they passed.

... The office was closed in a twinkling, and the clerk, with the long ends of his white comforter dangling below his waist (for he boasted no great-coat), went down a slide on Cornhill, at the end of a lane of boys, twenty times, in honour of its being Christmas-eve, and then ran home to Camden Town as hard as he could pelt, to play at blindman's buff.

Now, it is a fact, that there was nothing at all particular about the knocker on the door, except that it was very large. It is also a fact, that Scrooge had seen it, night and morning, during his whole residence in that place; also that Scrooge had as little of what is called fancy about him as any man in the city of London, even including—which is a bold word—the corporation, aldermen, and livery. Let it also be borne in mind that Scrooge had not bestowed one thought on Marley, since his last mention of his seven-years' dead partner that afternoon. And then let any man explain to me, if he can, how it happened that Scrooge, having his key in the lock of the door, saw in the knocker, without its undergoing any intermediate process of change—not a knocker, but Marley's face.

Upon its coming in, the dying flame leaped up, as though it cried, "I know him; Marley's Ghost!" and fell again. The same face: the very same. Marley in his pigtail, usual waistcoat, tights and boots; the tassels on the latter bristling, like his pigtail, and his coat-skirts, and the hair upon his head. The chain he drew was clasped about his middle. It was long, and wound about him like a tail; and it was made (for Scrooge observed it closely) of cashboxes, keys, padlocks, ledgers, deeds, and heavy purses wrought in steel. His body was transparent; so that Scrooge, observing him, and looking through his waistcoat, could see the two buttons on his coat behind.

Scrooge followed to the window: desperate in his curiosity. He looked out. The air was filled with phantoms, wandering hither and thither in restless haste, and moaning as they went. Every one of them wore chains like Marley's Ghost; some few (they might be guilty governments) were linked together; none were free. Many had been personally known to Scrooge in their lives. He had been quite familiar with one old ghost, in a white waistcoat, with a monstrous iron safe attached to its ankle, who cried piteously at being unable to assist a wretched woman with an infant, whom it saw below, upon a doorstep. The misery with them all was, clearly, that they sought to interfere, for good, in human matters, and had lost the power for ever.

It was a strange figure—like a child: yet not
so like a child as like an old man, viewed through
some supernatural medium, which gave him
the appearance of having receded from the view,
and being diminished to a child's proportions.
Its hair, which hung about its neck and down its
back, was white as if with age; and yet the face had
not a wrinkle in it, and the tenderest bloom was on
the skin. The arms were very long and muscular;
the hands the same, as if its hold were of uncommon
strength. Its legs and feet, most delicately formed,
were, like those upper members, bare ...
But the strangest thing about it was, that from
the crown of its head there sprung a bright clear
jet of light, by which all this was visible; and which
was doubtless the occasion of its using, in its duller
moments, a great extinguisher for a cap, which
it now held under its arm.

As the words were spoken, they passed through the wall, and stood upon an open country road, with fields on either hand. The city had entirely vanished. Not a vestige of it was to be seen. The darkness and the mist had vanished with it, for it was a clear, cold, winter day, with snow upon the ground.

... a mansion of dull red brick, with a little
weathercock-surmounted cupola, on the roof,
and a bell hanging in it. It was a large house,
but one of broken fortunes; for the spacious offices
were little used, their walls were damp and mossy,
their windows broken, and their gates decayed.
Fowls clucked and strutted in the stables; and the
coach-houses and sheds were over-run with grass.
Nor was it more retentive of its ancient state, within;
for entering the dreary hall, and glancing through
the open doors of many rooms, they found them
poorly furnished, cold, and vast.

They went, the Ghost and Scrooge, across the hall, to a door at the back of the house. It opened before them, and disclosed a long, bare, melancholy room, made barer still by lines of plain deal forms and desks. At one of these a lonely boy was reading near a feeble fire; and Scrooge sat down upon a form, and wept to see his poor forgotten self as he had used to be.

Suddenly a man in foreign garments: wonderfully
real and distinct to look at: stood outside the window,
with an axe stuck in his belt, and leading by the
bridle an ass laden with wood.

"Why, it's Ali Baba!" Scrooge exclaimed in ecstasy.
"It's dear old honest Ali Baba! Yes, yes, I know.
One Christmas-time when yonder solitary child
was left here all alone, he did come, for the first time,
just like that. Poor boy! And Valentine,"
said Scrooge, "and his wild brother, Orson; there
they go! And what's his name, who was put down
in his drawers, asleep, at the gate of Damascus;
don't you see him? And the Sultan's Groom turned
upside down by the Genii: there he is upon his head!
Serve him right! I'm glad of it. What business
had he to be married to the Princess?"

... in the hall appeared the schoolmaster himself, who glared on Master Scrooge with a ferocious condescension, and threw him into a dreadful state of mind by shaking hands with him.
He then conveyed him and his sister into the veriest old well of a shivering best-parlour that ever was seen, where the maps upon the wall, and the celestial and terrestrial globes in the windows, were waxy with cold.

And there was cake, and there was negus, and there was a great piece of Cold Roast, and there was a great piece of Cold Boiled, and there were mince-pies, and plenty of beer.

... when the fiddler (an artful dog, mind!
The sort of man who knew his business better than
you or I could have told it him!) struck up "Sir Roger
de Coverley." Then old Fezziwig stood out to dance
with Mrs. Fezziwig. Top couple, too; with a good stiff
piece of work cut out for them; three or four
and twenty pair of partners; people who were not
to be trifled with; people who would dance,
and had no notion of walking.

... again Scrooge saw himself. He was older now; a man in the prime of life. His face had not the harsh and rigid lines of later years; but it had begun to wear the signs of care and avarice. There was an eager, greedy, restless motion in the eye, which showed the passion that had taken root, and where the shadow of the growing tree would fall.

He was not alone, but sat by the side of a fair young girl in a mourning dress: in whose eyes there were tears, which sparkled in the light that shone out of the Ghost of Christmas Past.

"It matters little," she said softly. "To you, very little. Another idol has displaced me; and, if it can cheer and comfort you in time to come as I would have tried to do, I have no just cause to grieve."

"What Idol has displaced you?" he rejoined.

"A golden one."

They were in another scene and place; a room,
not very large or handsome, but full of comfort.
Near to the winter fire sat a beautiful young girl,
so like that last that Scrooge believed it was the
same, until he saw her, now a comely matron, sitting
opposite her daughter. The noise in this Room was
perfectly tumultuous, for there were more children
there, than Scrooge in his agitated state of mind
could count; and, unlike the celebrated herd in
the poem, they were not forty children conducting
themselves like one, but every child was conducting
itself like forty. The consequences were uproarious
beyond belief; but no one seemed to care; on the
contrary, the mother and daughter laughed heartily,
and enjoyed it very much; and the latter, soon
beginning to mingle in the sports, got pillaged
by the young brigands most ruthlessly.

It was his own room. There was no doubt about that. But it had undergone a surprising transformation. The walls and ceiling were so hung with living green, that it looked a perfect grove; from every part of which bright gleaming berries glistened. The crisp leaves of holly, mistletoe, and ivy reflected back the light, as if so many little mirrors had been scattered there; and such a mighty blaze went roaring up the chimney as that dull petrifaction of a hearth had never known in Scrooge's time, or Marley's, or for many and many a winter season gone. Heaped up on the floor, to form a kind of throne, were turkeys, geese, game, poultry, brawn, great joints of meat, sucking-pigs, long wreaths of sausages, mince-pies, plum-puddings, barrels of oysters, red-hot chestnuts, cherry-cheeked apples, juicy oranges, luscious pears, immense twelfth-cakes, and seething bowls of punch, that made the chamber dim with their delicious steam. In easy state upon this couch there sat a jolly Giant, glorious to see; who bore a glowing torch, in shape not unlike Plenty's horn, and held it up, high up, to shed its light on Scrooge as he came peeping round the door.

"Touch my robe!" Scrooge did as he was told, and held it fast. Holly, mistletoe, red berries, ivy, turkeys, geese, game, poultry, brawn, meat, pigs, sausages, oysters, pies, puddings, fruit, and punch, all vanished instantly. So did the room, the fire, the ruddy glow, the hour of night, and they stood in the city streets on Christmas morning, where (for the weather was severe) the people made a rough, but brisk and not unpleasant kind of music, in scraping the snow from the pavement in front of their dwellings, and from the tops of their houses, whence it was mad delight to the boys to see it come plumping down into the road below, and splitting into artificial little snow-storms.

For, the people who were shovelling away on the housetops were jovial and full of glee; calling out to one another from the parapets, and now and then exchanging a facetious snowball—better-natured missile far than many a wordy jest—laughing heartily if it went right, and not less heartily if it went wrong. The poulterers' shops were still half open, and the fruiterers' were radiant in their glory.

But soon the steeples called good people all to
church and chapel, and away they came, flocking
through the streets in their best clothes, and with
their gayest faces. And at the same time there
emerged, from scores of by-streets, lanes,
and nameless turnings, innumerable people,
carrying their dinners to the bakers' shops.
The sight of these poor revellers appeared to interest
the Spirit very much, for he stood with Scrooge
beside him in a baker's doorway, and, taking off
the covers as their bearers passed, sprinkled incense
on their dinners from his torch. And it was a very
uncommon kind of torch, for once or twice, when
there were angry words between some dinner-
carriers who had jostled each other, he shed a few
drops of water on them from it, and their good-
humour was restored directly. For they said,
it was a shame to quarrel upon Christmas-day.
And so it was! God love it, so it was!

In came little Bob, the father, with at least three feet
of comforter, exclusive of the fringe, hanging down
before him; and his threadbare clothes darned up
and brushed to look seasonable; and Tiny Tim
upon his shoulder. Alas for Tiny Tim, he bore
a little crutch, and had his limbs supported
by an iron frame!

Such a bustle ensued that you might have thought a goose the rarest of all birds; a feathered phenomenon, to which a black swan was a matter of course--and, in truth, it was something very like it in that house. Mrs. Cratchit made the gravy (ready beforehand in a little saucepan) hissing hot; Master Peter mashed the potatoes with incredible vigour; Miss Belinda sweetened up the apple sauce; Martha dusted the hot plates; Bob took Tiny Tim beside him in a tiny corner at the table; the two young Cratchits set chairs for everybody, not forgetting themselves, and, mounting guard upon their posts, crammed spoons into their mouths, lest they should shriek for goose before their turn came to be helped. At last the dishes were set on, and grace was said. It was succeeded by a breathless pause, as Mrs. Cratchit, looking slowly all along the carving-knife, prepared to plunge it in the breast; but when she did, and when the long-expected gush of stuffing issued forth, one murmur of delight arose all round the board, and even Tiny Tim, excited by the two young Cratchits, beat on the table with the handle of his knife, and feebly cried Hurrah!

Hallo! A great deal of steam! The pudding was out of the copper. A smell like a washing-day! That was the cloth. A smell like an eating-house and a pastrycook's next door to each other, with a laundress's next door to that! That was the pudding! In half a minute Mrs. Cratchit entered—flushed, but smiling proudly—with the pudding, like a speckled cannon-ball, so hard and firm, blazing in half of half-a-quartern of ignited brandy, and bedight with Christmas holly stuck into the top.

"God bless us every one!" said Tiny Tim,
the last of all.

He sat very close to his father's side, upon his little
stool. Bob held his withered little hand in his, as if he
loved the child, and wished to keep him by his side,
and dreaded that he might be taken from him.

"Mr. Scrooge!" said Bob. "I'll give you Mr. Scrooge, the Founder of the Feast!"

"The Founder of the Feast, indeed!" cried Mrs. Cratchit, reddening. "I wish I had him here. I'd give him a piece of my mind to feast upon, and I hope he'd have a good appetite for it."

"My dear," said Bob, "the children! Christmas-day."

"It should be Christmas-day, I am sure," said she, "on which one drinks the health of such an odious, stingy, hard, unfeeling man as Mr. Scrooge. You know he is, Robert! Nobody knows it better than you do, poor fellow!"

There was nothing of high mark in this. They were not a handsome family; they were not well dressed; their shoes were far from being waterproof; their clothes were scanty; and Peter might have known, and very likely did, the inside of a pawn-broker's. But they were happy, grateful, pleased with one another, and contented with the time; and when they faded, and looked happier yet in the bright sprinklings of the Spirit's torch at parting, Scrooge had his eye upon them, and especially on Tiny Tim, until the last.

By this time it was getting dark, and snowing pretty heavily; and as Scrooge and the Spirit went along the streets, the brightness of the roaring fires in kitchens, parlours, and all sorts of rooms was wonderful. Here, the flickering of the blaze showed preparations for a cosy dinner, with hot plates baking through and through before the fire, and deep red curtains, ready to be drawn to shut out cold and darkness ... Here, again, were shadows on the window blinds of guests assembling; and there a group of handsome girls, all hooded and fur-booted, and all chattering at once, tripped lightly off to some near neighbour's house; where, woe upon the single man who saw them enter—artful witches, well they knew it—in a glow!

The Spirit did not tarry here, but bade Scrooge
hold his robe, and, passing on above the moor, sped
whither? Not to sea? To sea. To Scrooge's horror,
looking back, he saw the last of the land, a frightful
range of rocks, behind them; and his ears were
deafened by the thundering of water, as it rolled
and roared, and raged among the dreadful caverns
it had worn, and fiercely tried to undermine
the earth.

The way he went after that plump sister in the lace tucker was an outrage on the credulity of human nature. Knocking down the fire-irons, tumbling over the chairs, bumping up against the piano, smothering himself amongst the curtains, wherever she went, there went he! He always knew where the plump sister was. He wouldn't catch anybody else. If you had fallen up against him (as some of them did) on purpose, he would have made a feint of endeavouring to seize you, which would have been an affront to your understanding, and would instantly have sidled off in the direction of the plump sister. She often cried out that it wasn't fair; and it really was not.

From the foldings of its robe it brought two children;
wretched, abject, frightful, hideous, miserable.
They knelt down at its feet, and clung upon the
outside of its garment.

"Oh, Man! look here! Look, look, down here!"
exclaimed the Ghost.

They were a boy and girl. Yellow, meagre, ragged,
scowling, wolfish; but prostrate, too, in their
humility. Where graceful youth should have filled
their features out, and touched them with its freshest
tints, a stale and shrivelled hand, like that of age,
had pinched, and twisted them, and pulled them into
shreds. Where angels might have sat enthroned,
devils lurked, and glared out menacing. No change,
no degradation, no perversion of humanity,
in any grade, through all the mysteries of wonderful
creation, has monsters half so horrible and dread.

It was shrouded in a deep black garment, which concealed its head, its face, its form, and left nothing of it visible save one outstretched hand. But for this it would have been difficult to detach its figure from the night, and separate it from the darkness by which it was surrounded. He felt that it was tall and stately when it came beside him, and that its mysterious presence filled him with a solemn dread. He knew no more, for the Spirit neither spoke nor moved.

"Why, what was the matter with him?" asked a third, taking a vast quantity of snuff out of a very large snuff-box. "I thought he'd never die."

"God knows," said the first with a yawn.

"What has he done with his money?" asked a red-faced gentleman with a pendulous excrescence on the end of his nose, that shook like the gills of a turkey-cock.

"I haven't heard," said the man with the large chin, yawning again. "Left it to his company, perhaps. He hasn't left it to me. That's all I know."

Scrooge and the Phantom came into the presence
of this man, just as a woman with a heavy bundle
slunk into the shop. But she had scarcely entered,
when another woman, similarly laden, came in too,
and she was closely followed by a man in faded
black, who was no less startled by the sight of them
than they had been upon the recognition of each
other. After a short period of blank astonishment,
in which the old man with the pipe had joined them,
they all three burst into a laugh.

"Spirit!" said Scrooge, shuddering from head to foot. "I see, I see. The case of this unhappy man might be my own. My life tends that way now. Merciful Heaven, what is this?"

He recoiled in terror, for the scene had changed, and now he almost touched a bed: a bare, uncurtained bed: on which, beneath a ragged sheet, there lay a something covered up, which, though it was dumb, announced itself in awful language.

The room was very dark, too dark to be observed with any accuracy, though Scrooge glanced round it in obedience to a secret impulse, anxious to know what kind of room it was. A pale light, rising in the outer air, fell straight upon the bed: and on it, plundered and bereft, unwatched, unwept, uncared for, was the body of this man.

He sat down to the dinner that had been hoarding for him by the fire, and, when she asked him faintly what news (which was not until after a long silence), he appeared embarrassed how to answer.

"Is it good," she said, "or bad?" to help him.

"Bad," he answered.

"We are quite ruined?"

"No. There is hope yet, Caroline."

"If he relents," she said, amazed, "there is! Nothing is past hope, if such a miracle has happened."

"He is past relenting," said her husband. "He is dead."

"Yes, my dear," returned Bob. "I wish you could have gone. It would have done you good to see how green a place it is. But you'll see it often. I promised him that I would walk there on a Sunday. My little, little child!" cried Bob. "My little child!"

He broke down all at once. He couldn't help it. If he could have helped it, he and his child would have been farther apart, perhaps, than they were.

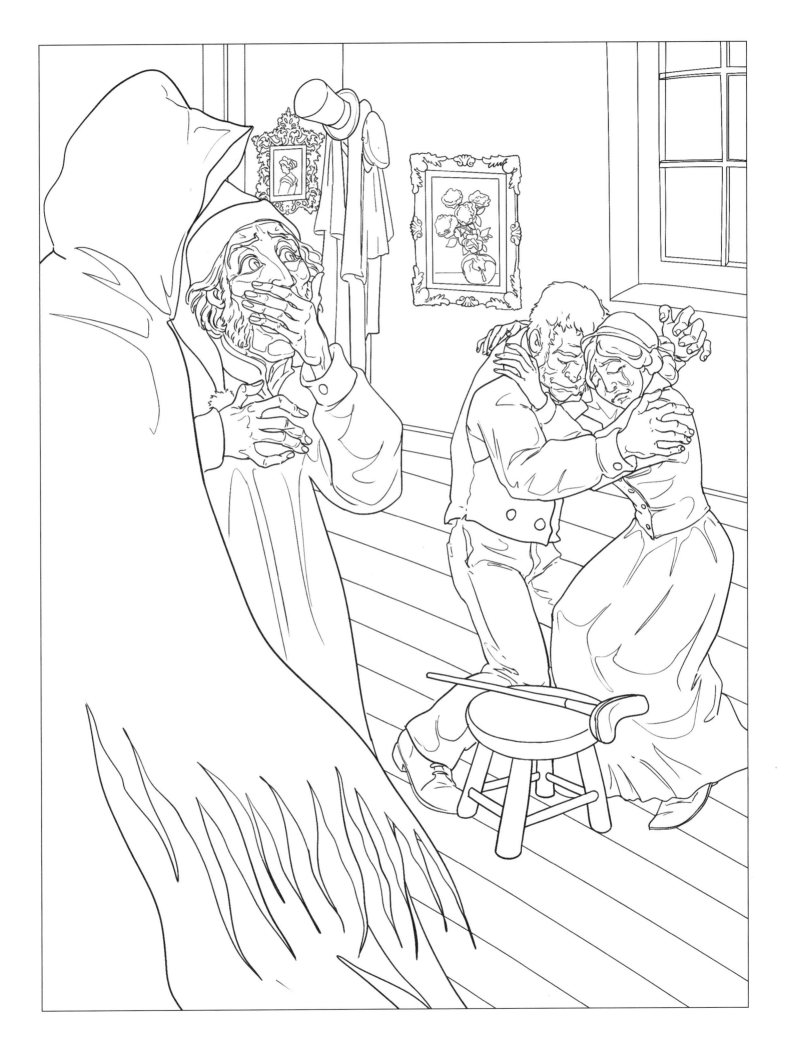

"Men's courses will foreshadow certain ends,
to which, if persevered in, they must lead,"
said Scrooge. "But if the courses be departed from,
the ends will change. Say it is thus with what
you show me!"

The Spirit was immovable as ever.

Scrooge crept towards it, trembling as he went;
and, following the finger, read upon the stone
of the neglected grave his own name,
EBENEZER SCROOGE.

He was checked in his transports by the churches
ringing out the lustiest peals he had ever heard.
Clash, clang, hammer; ding, dong, bell. Bell, dong,
ding; hammer, clang, clash! Oh, glorious, glorious!

The chuckle with which he said this, and the chuckle with which he paid for the Turkey, and the chuckle with which he paid for the cab, and the chuckle with which he recompensed the boy, were only to be exceeded by the chuckle with which he sat down breathless in his chair again, and chuckled till he cried.

"A merry Christmas, Bob!" said Scrooge with
an earnestness that could not be mistaken, as he
clapped him on the back. "A merrier Christmas,
Bob, my good fellow, than I have given you for many
a year! I'll raise your salary, and endeavour to assist
your struggling family, and we will discuss your
affairs this very afternoon, over a Christmas bowl
of smoking bishop, Bob! Make up the fires and buy
another coal-scuttle before you dot another i,
Bob Cratchit!"

Scrooge was better than his word. He did it all, and infinitely more; and to Tiny Tim, who did NOT die, he was a second father. He became as good a friend, as good a master, and as good a man as the good old City knew, or any other good old city, town, or borough in the good old world. Some people laughed to see the alteration in him, but he let them laugh, and little heeded them; for he was wise enough to know that nothing ever happened on this globe, for good, at which some people did not have their fill of laughter in the outset; and, knowing that such as these would be blind anyway, he thought it quite as well that they should wrinkle up their eyes in grins as have the malady in less attractive forms. His own heart laughed: and that was quite enough for him.